HEALING & REDEMPTION

Rebuilding with Purpose

Sheresse Winford

Struggles to Success
A Series of Hope and Inspiration

Struggles to Success
A Series of Hope and Inspiration

® Copyright 2025. Sheresse Winford.

All rights reserved. No portion of this book may be reproduced by mechanical, photographic, or electronic process, nor may it be stored in a retrieval system, transmitted in any form or otherwise be copied for public or private use without written permission of the copyright owner.

For more information contact:
www.figfactormedia.com

Cover Design and Layout by DG Marco Antonio Álvarez Rodríguez
Printed in the United States of America

ISBN: 978-1-961600-45-4

Library of Congress Control Number: 2024921294

HEALING & REDEMPTION

Rebuilding with Purpose

Dedication

To my siblings, Katrice Winford, Andrea Winford, Lenia Winford, and Michael Nimock.

Thank you for believing in me and never giving up on me, even when the journey was difficult. Your love, encouragement, and support have been a constant source of strength. I am forever grateful for the role each of you has played in my life, the love you have shown me, and for the bond we share.

Table of Contents

6   Acknowledgments
8   Introduction

11 Chapter 1: A Journey Toward Healing
15 Chapter 2: Lessons in Letting Go
19 Chapter 3: The Gift of Perspective
23 Chapter 4: Finding Strength in New Beginnings
27 Chapter 5: Turning Setbacks into Strength
31 Chapter 6: Rising Above Challenges
35 Chapter 7: Building New Foundations
39 Chapter 8: The Freedom of Self-Acceptance
43 Chapter 9: The Power of Reconciliation
47 Chapter 10: Discovering Inner Strength
51 Chapter 11: Embracing Hope and Purpose
55 Chapter 12: Redemption Through Empowerment

62 About the Author

Acknowledgments

To *A Safe Haven Foundation*,

Thank you for providing me with a sanctuary to grow and blossom into the person I was meant to be. Your unlimited resources and programs, along with your encouragement, have helped guide me into a new way of life. I will forever be thankful for your support and the beautiful blessing you've been in my journey. You've given me hope, strength, and the tools to flourish, and for that, I am eternally grateful.

Introduction

Healing and Redemption: Rebuilding with Purpose is the powerful conclusion to Sheresse Winford's inspiring trilogy, *Struggles to Success: A Series of Hope and Inspiration*. In this final book, Sheresse reflects on her journey of healing, resilience, and the courage it took to rebuild her life after years of hardship. It's a story of transformation that reminds us of the strength we have within to rise, rebuild, and thrive.

This book delves into the process of turning pain into power, mistakes into milestones, and struggles into stepping stones for growth. Sheresse's story is raw and unflinchingly honest yet genuinely hopeful. She takes us through the highs and lows of her path to redemption, exploring the challenges she faced as she fought to reclaim her life. From rebuilding fractured relationships to rediscovering her purpose, Sheresse's journey is a testament to the resilience of the human spirit.

Through each chapter, Sheresse shares the lessons she learned as she rebuilt her foundation. Her journey began with earning her GED and pursuing her passions in cosmetology, cooking, and computer technology—steps that symbolized her commitment to creating a future she could be proud of. These achievements were more than academic milestones. They were proof of her inner strength and determination to rewrite her story.

But *Healing and Redemption* isn't just about personal victories. It's also about the power of community, compassion, and the role that others play in our healing. Sheresse recounts the kindness she received from individuals like Tammy and Jerome, whose support helped her find stability and hope. Their belief in her, coupled with her own growing self-belief, reminded her of the importance of connection and the strength that comes from leaning on others.

At its core, this book is a call to action for anyone who has ever felt defeated by life's challenges. Sheresse's story encourages you to reflect on your own life, using her experiences as a guide to find healing and purpose. Each chapter is paired with a reflective question, inviting you to consider how your setbacks can become opportunities for growth. These questions make *Healing and Redemption* more than just a memoir—it's a tool for personal transformation.

Sheresse's journey teaches us that redemption is not about perfection but progress. It's about forgiving yourself, embracing your past, and using it as fuel for a brighter future. She shows us that no matter how far we've fallen, we all have the power to rebuild our lives with purpose and intention.

Healing and Redemption brings Sheresse's trilogy to a close with a message of hope, strength, and the limitless potential within each of us. This book will inspire you to face life's challenges with courage and to embrace the beauty of rebuilding.

Chapter 1:

A Journey Toward Healing

Life is unpredictable—a blend of joys and struggles that often seems unfair. My path has been marked with challenges, but each stumble taught me something I couldn't have learned otherwise. Healing, I've found, isn't a straight road. It's winding, bumpy, and filled with moments that force you to look within.

I had a loving family growing up, but life wasn't easy. My father's struggles with alcoholism made home unpredictable. On his good days, he was the dad who helped with homework and played games. On the bad days, he was someone I didn't recognize, someone whose actions left scars deeper than words could explain. Those moments shaped me in ways I didn't fully understand then, but even in the hardest times, I found love and resilience in my mother, siblings, and community.

When my parents separated, I felt lost. My father had been my anchor, even with his flaws. His absence left a void, and I didn't know how to process it. I turned inward, carrying pain I didn't yet have the tools to heal. It wasn't until years later, after losing him entirely, that I realized the strength his struggles had ignited in me.

Healing began when I stopped looking for answers outside myself. I started to see every challenge as an opportunity to rebuild. My mother's steady commitment to us, despite her hardships, showed me the power of perseverance. Even our neighbors—kind, generous people who stepped in during difficult times—taught me the importance of community and compassion.

Healing isn't a finish line you cross— it's a lifelong journey. Every time I faced a setback, I learned something new about myself. I've learned to forgive myself for my mistakes and to embrace the lessons they've brought. Each step forward, no matter how small, is a victory.

We all have a story of falling and rising again. It's those stories that shape us, that push us to grow, and that remind us how strong we truly are.

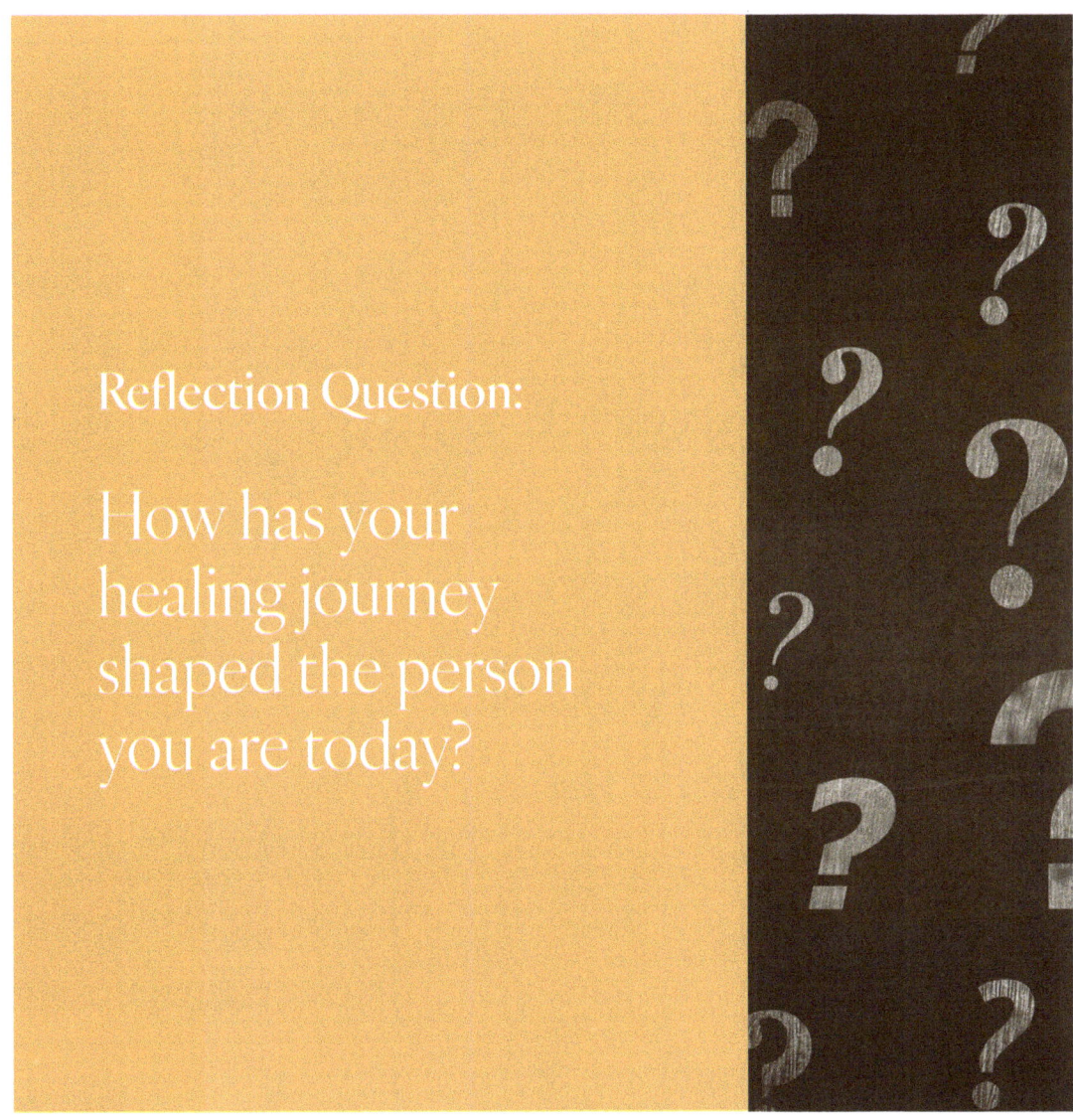

Reflection Question:

How has your healing journey shaped the person you are today?

Chapter 2:

Lessons in Letting Go

My teenage years were a whirlwind of rebellion and self-discovery. It felt like I was constantly wrestling with life's pressures, trying to carve out a space where I could just breathe. At the time, skipping school, hanging out with the wrong crowd, and sneaking alcohol felt like liberation. But those fleeting moments of freedom came with a cost that I didn't fully understand until later.

By the time I reached 11th grade, I had fallen so far behind in school that I couldn't catch up. Dropping out felt like the only option. It wasn't just the academics. The lies I told to cover up my mistakes had strained my relationship with my mother, someone who wanted the best for me, even if I couldn't see it then. I blamed her for being too strict but looking back, I see her rules were intended to protect me from myself.

Leaving school wasn't easy, but it forced me to start looking at my life differently. It became a lesson in letting go—of rigid expectations, the need to control everything, and, eventually, my guilt. Stepping away from the structure I had fought against allowed me to explore what I truly wanted from life. I began to realize that letting go didn't mean giving up—it meant making space for something new.

Each misstep taught me resilience and self-awareness. I started to see the value in learning from mistakes rather than being defined by them. Letting go wasn't just about moving on from the past—it was about learning to trust the process, even when I couldn't see where it would lead.

Those years weren't easy, but they laid the foundation for the growth that came later. Letting go of who I thought I should be allowed me to discover who I was meant to become.

Reflection Question:

How can the challenges in your life become stepping stones toward growth?

Chapter 3:
———
The Gift of Perspective

Running away at 16 felt like my only escape. I craved freedom from rules I didn't understand and a life that felt suffocating. When Tammy welcomed me into her home, I thought I had found the peace I was searching for. She gave me a safe space and a sense of belonging I hadn't felt in years, but peace is fragile, and when the police came, it all fell apart.

Watching Tammy, a woman who had shown me only kindness, be arrested for helping me was devastating. I'll never forget the sound of her children crying as they watched their mother being taken away. At that moment, guilt crashed over me like a tidal wave. My actions hadn't just affected me—they had impacted others in ways I never anticipated.

That experience changed me. It was a harsh lesson in accountability. Tammy's generosity was a reminder that there are good people in the world, people willing to help even when it's risky. It also taught me about the ripple effect of my choices. Every action has consequences, and those consequences often touch the lives of others in ways we can't foresee.

Perspective is a gift. It helps you see beyond your own pain and recognize the impact you have on others. Tammy's selflessness taught me that life is about connection, lifting others up, and finding the strength to do better when you know better.

As painful as that chapter of my life was, it became a turning point. It opened my eyes to the importance of gratitude and accountability. I learned to appreciate the people who stood by me and was determined to become someone who honored their faith in me.

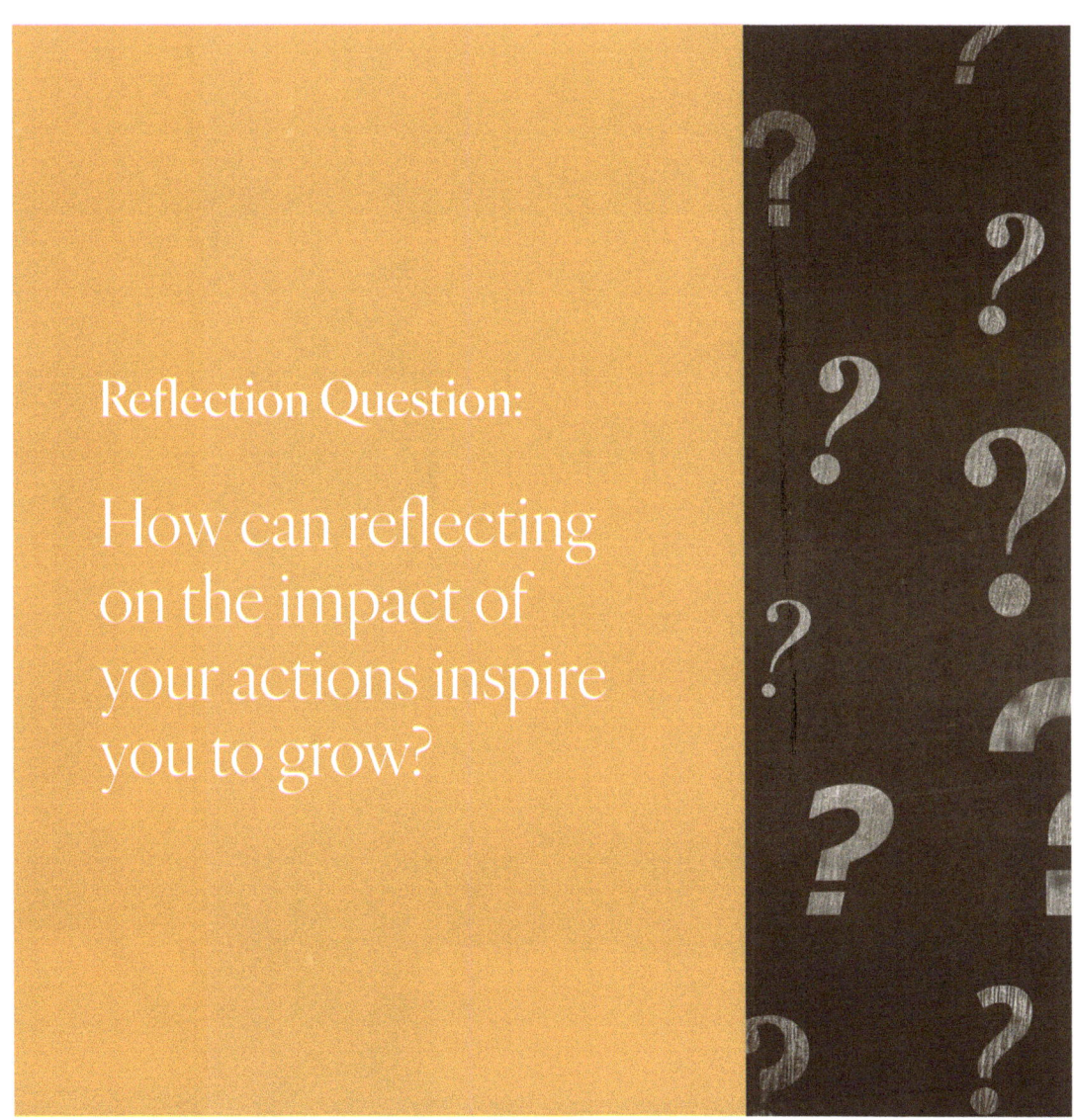

Reflection Question:

How can reflecting on the impact of your actions inspire you to grow?

Chapter 4:

Finding Strength in New Beginnings

When I ran away for the second time, I felt like there was no turning back. I couldn't face going home again, and Tammy, understandably, couldn't take me in after what had happened. I didn't know where to go or what to do next. That's when Jerome stepped into my life. He wasn't just kind—he believed in me when I didn't believe in myself.

Jerome gave me more than a place to stay—he gave me hope. He paid the rent, bought furniture, and made me feel like I mattered. For the first time in a long time, I felt stable and secure, but Jerome didn't stop there. He encouraged me to pursue my GED, reminding me that I had the potential to create a better future. His faith in me became a spark that reignited my belief in myself.

The journey wasn't easy. I carried the weight of my past, the guilt, and the uncertainty about whether I could truly change. Slowly, I began to see that I was stronger than I realized. I started to take small steps toward rebuilding my life. Each milestone—studying for my GED, attending classes, imagining a future where I could be proud of myself—became proof of my resilience.

Jerome's support was a turning point. He showed me the power of having someone in your corner, someone who sees your potential even when you can't. His kindness taught me that sometimes, the first step toward healing is accepting help from others.

New beginnings aren't easy, and they don't erase the past, but they offer something invaluable—the chance to write a new story. Looking back, I see that those moments of starting over taught me strength, courage, and the importance of hope. They showed me that no matter how far you've fallen, you can always rise again.

Reflection Question:

How can the support of others inspire you to reach for your goals?

Chapter 5:

Turning Setbacks into Strength

Life has a way of humbling you when you least expect it. For me, one of those moments came with a setback that seemed insurmountable—imprisonment. The feeling of confinement wasn't just physical. It was emotional and mental, a stark reminder of how far I had strayed from the life I wanted.

At first, I couldn't see past the walls around me. Shame, regret, and anger consumed me. I felt trapped not only by my circumstances but also by the mistakes that had brought me there. As the days passed, though, something began to shift. I realized that while I couldn't change my past, I could shape my future.

Being forced to pause gave me time to reflect. I thought about what I wanted my life to look like and the steps I needed to take to get there. Slowly, I began to see my setback as an opportunity—a chance to rebuild from the ground up. It wasn't easy, and the road ahead seemed daunting, but I knew I had to start somewhere.

When I was released, I faced an entirely new set of challenges. Finding a job with a criminal record felt impossible, and the stigma followed me everywhere I went, but I refused to let it break me. I took on any work I could find, determined to prove that I was more than my mistakes.

Each small victory reminded me of my strength. Over time, I began to see my setbacks not as failures but as turning points. They forced me to confront who I was and pushed me toward who I wanted to become.

Looking back, I know those moments of adversity were some of the most transformative in my life. They taught me resilience, courage, and the power of starting over. Life will knock you down, but it's in getting back up that you discover your true strength.

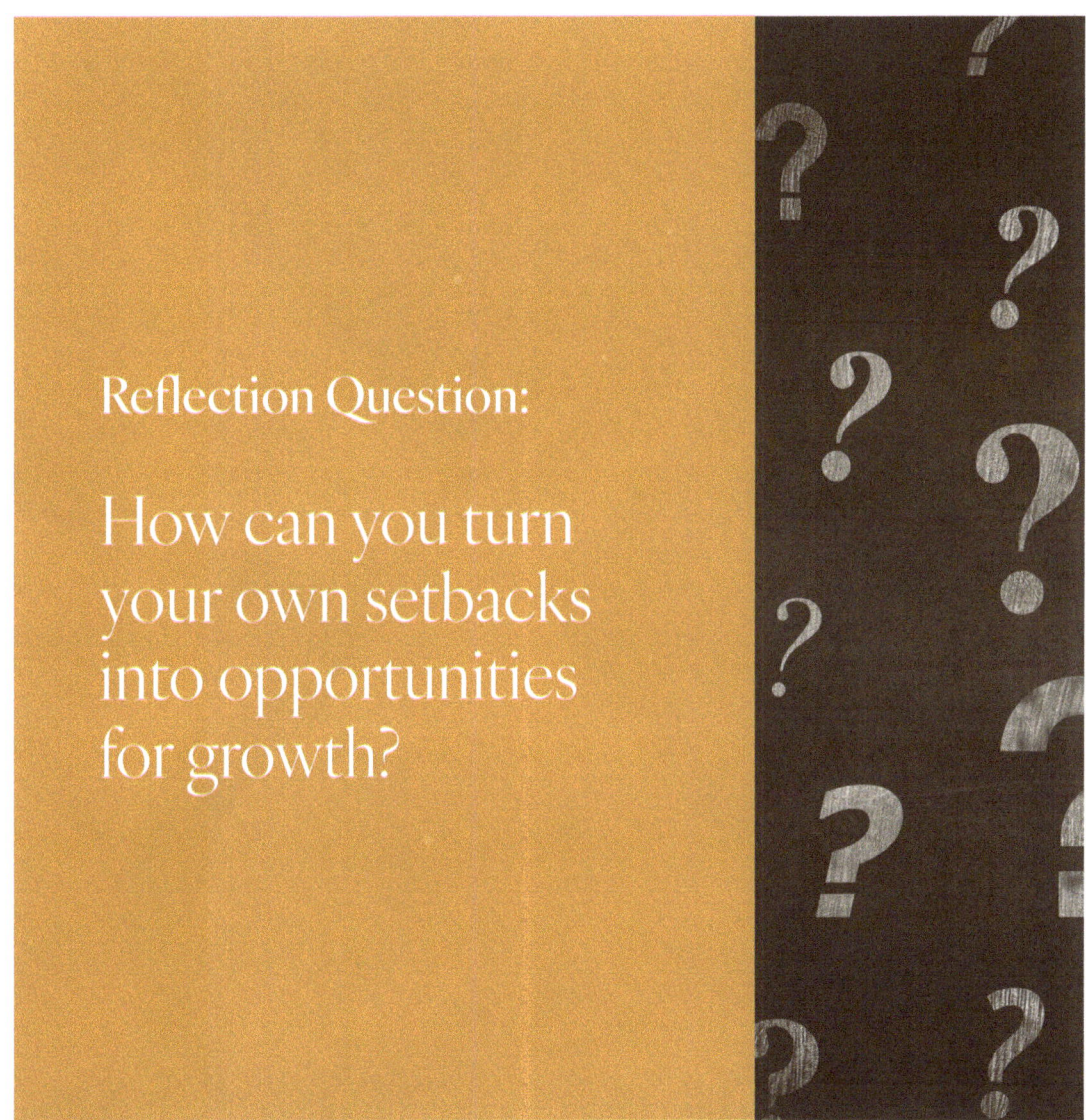

Reflection Question:

How can you turn your own setbacks into opportunities for growth?

Chapter 6:

Rising Above Challenges

Carrying a criminal record felt like an inescapable burden. Every job interview was a reminder of my mistakes, every rejection a blow to my self-worth. For a long time, I believed I was stuck—that my past had built walls I could never climb.

Life, however, has a way of teaching you lessons exactly when you're ready to learn them. I realized that no one else could define my future unless I allowed them to. I had to choose resilience over resignation. That decision wasn't easy, and it didn't come all at once. It started with small, deliberate actions—applying for jobs even when I knew the odds were against me and showing up even when I wanted to give up.

There were many "nos" before I finally got a "yes." My first opportunities weren't glamorous or what I had dreamed of, but they were the foundation that my success has been built upon. Each job and each new experience reminded me that I was more than my mistakes. I began to see challenges not as barriers but as opportunities to prove to myself that I could persevere.

Overcoming obstacles wasn't just about survival. It was about transformation. I learned to take ownership of my story. I stopped hiding from my past and started using it as fuel to push forward. Every hurdle I overcame made me stronger, more determined, and more aware of my own strength and resilience.

The challenges I faced shaped me in ways I couldn't have imagined. They taught me patience, persistence, and the importance of self-belief. Rising above didn't mean forgetting where I came from—it meant using those experiences to grow into the person I wanted to be.

Looking back, I'm grateful for the strength I found in those moments. They showed me that no obstacle is too great if you're willing to keep going, one step at a time.

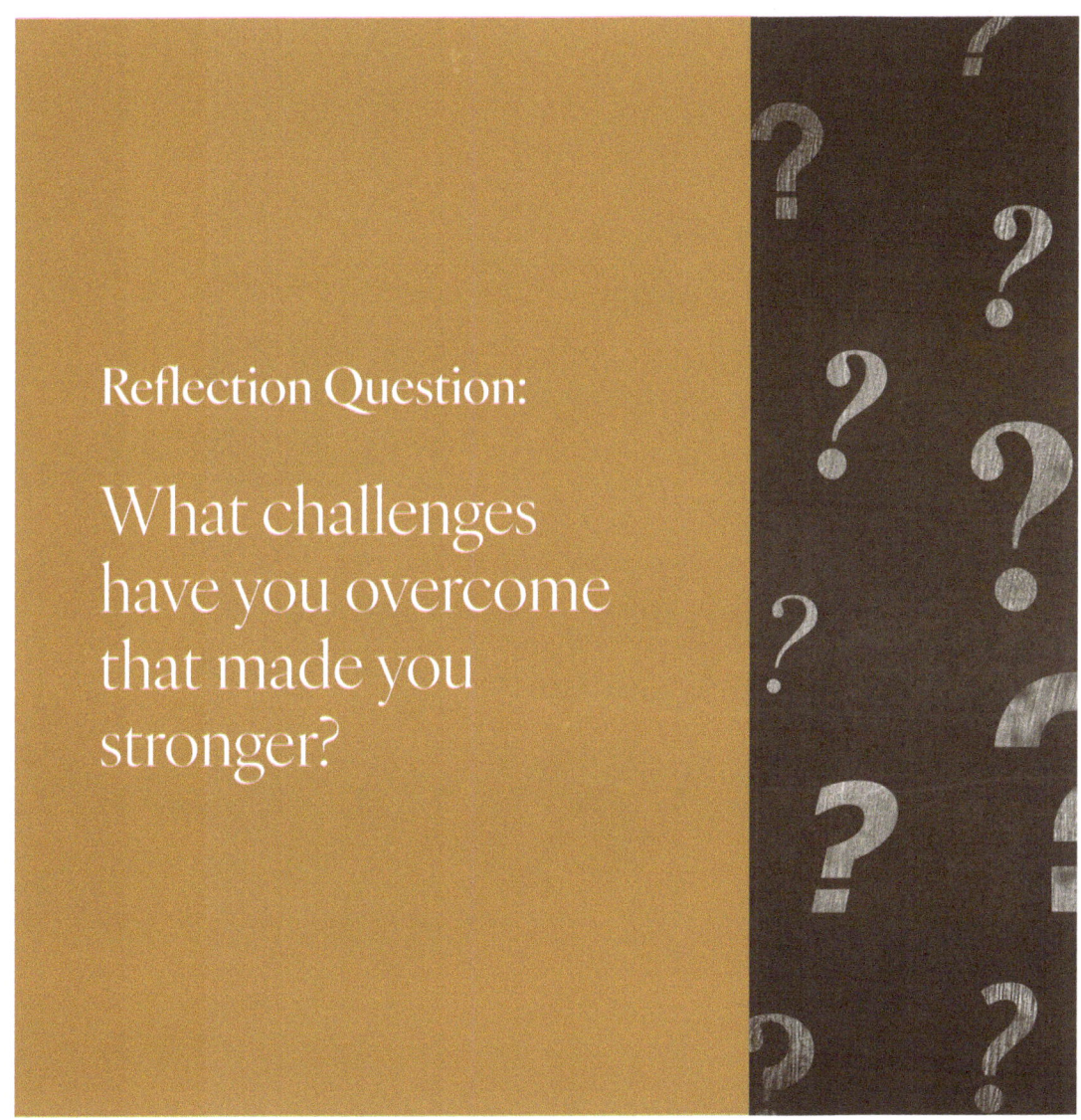

Reflection Question:

What challenges have you overcome that made you stronger?

Chapter 7:

Building New Foundations

For so long, I felt like my life was built on shaky ground. The choices I had made and the circumstances I faced all seemed to undermine any chance of stability, but I realized that if I wanted a better future, I had to start building a stronger foundation for myself.

Education became my first step. After earning my GED, I knew I couldn't stop there. I enrolled in culinary school, driven by my love for cooking. It wasn't easy balancing the demands of school and work, but every skill I learned felt like a building block for a brighter future. The nine months I spent earning my culinary certification taught me discipline and gave me a sense of accomplishment I hadn't felt in years.

However, my journey didn't end there. Next, I pursued a certification in computers—a field that intimidated me at first but soon became another turning point. Each course and each new skill reminded me that I was capable of growth. With every class I completed, I felt more empowered to create a life I could be proud of.

Learning wasn't only about gaining qualifications. It was about discovering my potential. It taught me that growth is a lifelong process, and every skill I acquired opened new doors. The joy of mastering something new gave me hope and purpose.

Building a strong foundation was also about more than education. It was about rebuilding my confidence and trust in myself. I learned that starting over doesn't mean you've failed—it means you're brave enough to try again.

Now, when I look back on those moments, I see them as the building blocks for my transformation. They were proof that even when life feels uncertain, we have the power to create something solid and lasting.

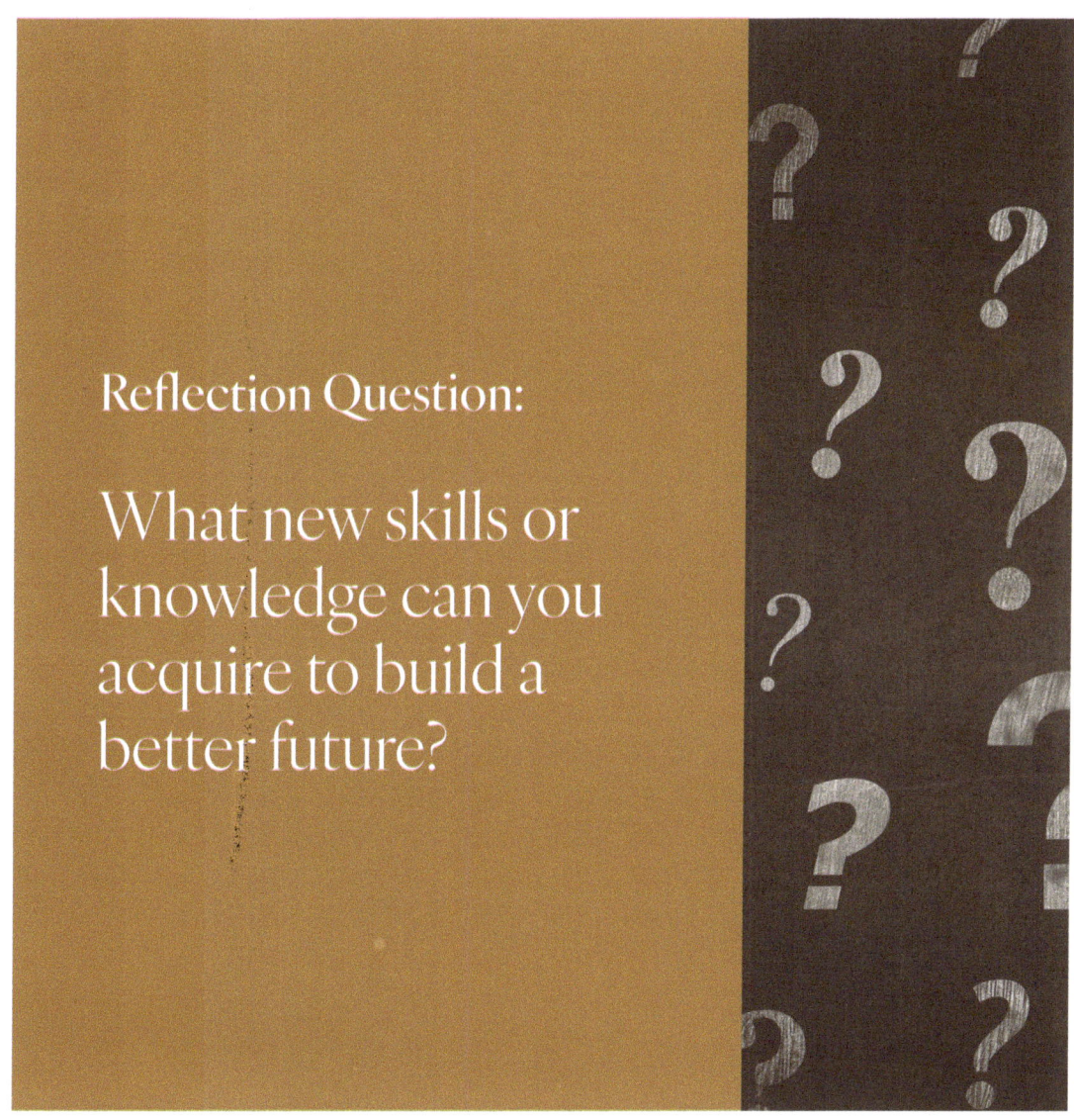

Reflection Question:

What new skills or knowledge can you acquire to build a better future?

Chapter 8:

The Freedom of Self-Acceptance

For the longest time, I carried the weight of my mistakes like a heavy chain around my neck. Every poor decision, every moment of weakness, seemed to define who I was. I thought if people knew the real me, they'd judge me, and worse, I couldn't stop judging myself. It wasn't until I learned the power of self-acceptance that I finally began to break free.

Accepting myself didn't come easily. It required me to face the parts of my story I wanted to forget. I had to confront the guilt I felt for the pain I'd caused my family, the shame of the paths I'd chosen, and the fear that I would never be enough. But through it all, I realized something life-changing. I didn't have to be perfect to be worthy of love and happiness.

Forgiveness was the key. First, I needed to forgive others—my father for his struggles with addiction and my mother for the choices I once blamed her for. Even more than that, I had to forgive myself. I had to stop replaying the moments where I felt I'd failed and start focusing on the lessons those moments had taught me.

Self-acceptance isn't about ignoring your flaws or pretending your mistakes didn't happen. It's about embracing the whole of who you are, flaws and all, and understanding that those flaws don't diminish your value. In fact, they can make you stronger and more compassionate.

When I finally let go of the guilt, it felt like I could breathe again. I realized that my past didn't have to define my future. By embracing who I was—every mistake and every victory—I found a sense of freedom I never thought possible.

Self-acceptance is a journey, not a destination, and each step toward embracing yourself brings a little more peace, a little more joy, and a lot more hope.

Reflection Question:

What steps can you take to forgive yourself and embrace self-acceptance?

Chapter 9:

The Power of Reconciliation

Rebuilding relationships has been one of the hardest yet most rewarding parts of my healing journey. For years, I held onto resentment and blame, especially toward my mother. I saw her rules as controlling, her punishments as unfair, and her decisions as the root of my struggles. It took time and a lot of reflection to see things differently.

Reconciliation doesn't happen overnight. It began with understanding—realizing that my mother wasn't perfect but that she loved me fiercely in the only way she knew how. Her strictness wasn't meant to stifle me. It was her way of protecting me from a world she knew could be unforgiving. Once I saw that, the walls I had built around my heart started to come down.

Reconnecting with my siblings was another part of this process. As kids, we shared everything—our laughter, our secrets, even our fears, but as life pulled us in different directions, those bonds began to fray. Healing those relationships required vulnerability and honesty. It meant admitting my own faults and being willing to hear theirs, too.

The most powerful lesson I've learned is that reconciliation isn't just about repairing the past. It's about building a better future. It's about creating space for understanding, for forgiveness, and for love. The conversations I've had with my family—some painful and others joyful—have brought us closer than I ever thought possible.

Reconciliation has also taught me that healing isn't just an individual journey—it's something we do together. When we mend our connections with others, we also mend parts of ourselves. The love and support I've found in my family have been some of the greatest sources of strength in my life.

The power of reconciliation lies in its ability to transform pain into connection and brokenness into wholeness. It reminds us that even the most strained relationships can find new life.

Reflection Question:

How can healing damaged relationships help you in your own journey?

Chapter 10:

Discovering Inner Strength

Strength is a word that gets thrown around a lot, but for me, it wasn't something I truly understood until life forced me to dig deep. It's easy to think of strength as something physical or visible, but I've learned that true strength often comes from within—quiet, steady, and resilient.

My life has had its fair share of challenges, and there were moments when I doubted whether I could handle what was being thrown my way. Losing my father, dropping out of school, facing the stigma of my mistakes—all of it felt overwhelming, but with each hardship, I discovered something incredible. I was stronger than I thought.

Inner strength isn't something you're born with. It's something you build. I started to see this when I began taking small steps to change my life. Earning my GED, pursuing certifications, and rebuilding my relationships weren't just external accomplishments—they were proof that I had the resilience to keep going, even when it was hard.

One of the most important lessons I've learned is that strength doesn't mean never feeling pain or fear. It means acknowledging those emotions and choosing to move forward anyway. It's about finding the courage to face your struggles head-on and the determination to keep trying, no matter how many times you stumble.

I also discovered that strength isn't just about surviving. It's about thriving. It's about taking the lessons life hands you and using them to grow into the person you want to be. Each challenge I faced helped me uncover a new layer of resilience, courage, and self-reliance.

Now, when I look back on the hardest moments of my life, I see them as the times when my inner strength was forged. They reminded me that no matter what comes my way, I have the power to rise above it.

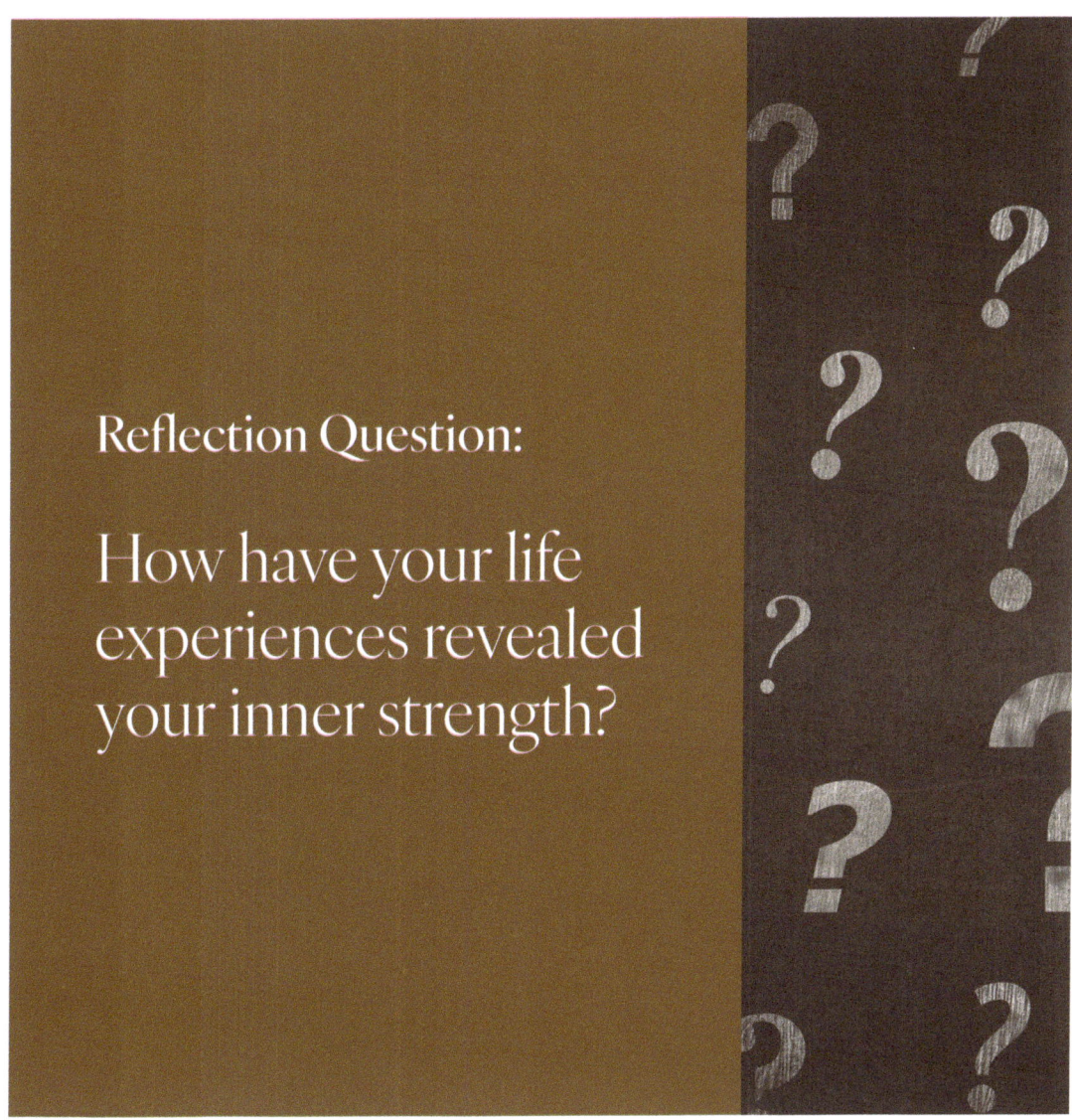

Reflection Question:

How have your life experiences revealed your inner strength?

Chapter 11:

Embracing Hope and Purpose

Hope has been my source of strength, even in the darkest times. It's what kept me going when everything else felt uncertain. Finding hope isn't always easy, though. Once you do, though, it's something you must hold onto, even when life gives you every reason to let go.

For me, hope began to take root when I started building a life I could be proud of. Earning certifications in culinary arts and computers wasn't just about gaining skills—it was about proving to myself that I was capable of more. Each accomplishment reminded me that I had a future worth fighting for, even if I couldn't always see it clearly.

Purpose came into focus as I began working in fields I loved. Cooking, in particular, became more than just a job. It was a way to create, to bring joy to others, and to feel connected to something bigger than myself. Finding work that aligned with my passions gave me a sense of fulfillment I hadn't experienced before.

Hope and purpose, I learned, go hand in hand. Hope gives you the strength to keep moving forward, and purpose gives you the direction to aim for. Together, they create a foundation for a life filled with meaning.

I've also learned that purpose doesn't have to be grand or world-changing. It can be found in the small, everyday moments—in the connections we make with others, in the work we do, and in the love we share. For me, purpose has been about using my experiences to grow, to give back, and to inspire others to find their own path forward.

Embracing hope and purpose has transformed the way I see my journey. It's shown me that no matter how many times life knocks you down, there's always a reason to get back up.

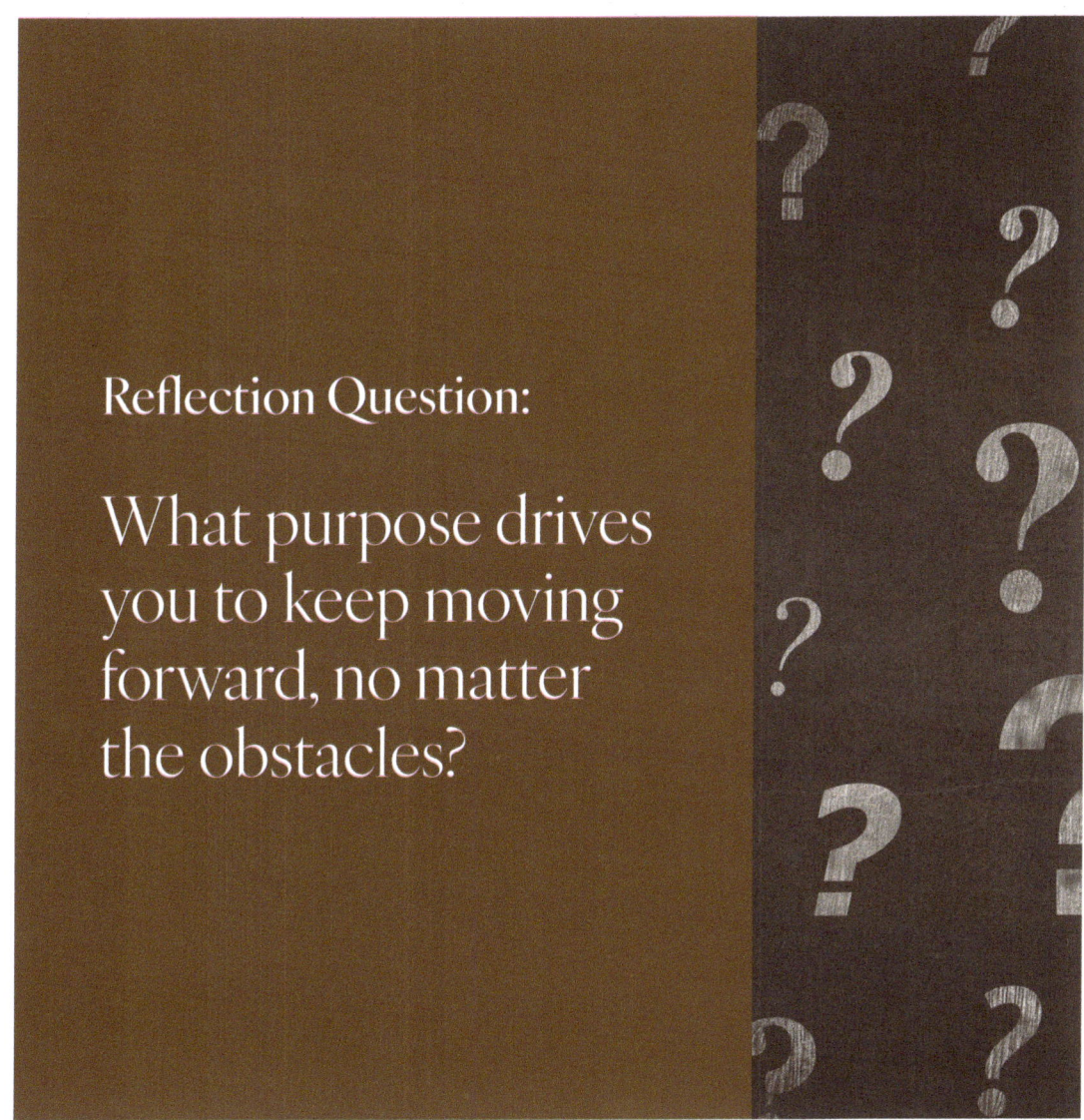

Reflection Question:

What purpose drives you to keep moving forward, no matter the obstacles?

Chapter 12:

Redemption Through Empowerment

Redemption is a powerful word. For me, it's about more than just overcoming my past—it's about stepping into my power and using my story to inspire others. Redemption isn't about forgetting where you've been. It's about transforming it into something meaningful and empowering.

Looking back, I see how far I've come. The mistakes, the setbacks, the moments of doubt—they were all part of a larger journey. Each challenge forced me to grow in ways I never thought possible. They taught me resilience, courage, and the importance of self-belief.

Yet, redemption didn't happen in isolation. It came from sharing my story, being honest about my struggles, and showing others that change is possible. I've learned that our experiences, no matter how painful, have the power to inspire and uplift others. By owning my story, I've found a sense of purpose and empowerment that I never imagined.

Empowerment, for me, is about taking control of your narrative. It's about refusing to be defined by your mistakes and instead using them as a foundation to build something better. It's about believing in yourself, even when the world doubts you, and proving to yourself that you are capable of greatness.

Redemption isn't only about personal transformation. It's about creating a ripple effect. By embracing my own journey, I've been able to encourage others to do the same. It's a reminder that we are all capable of growth, that no matter where we start, we have the power to change our lives—and the lives of those around us.

As I reflect on my journey, I'm filled with gratitude for the lessons I've learned and the strength I've gained. Redemption isn't the end of the story, though. It's the beginning of a new chapter—one filled with hope, purpose, and the determination to make a difference.

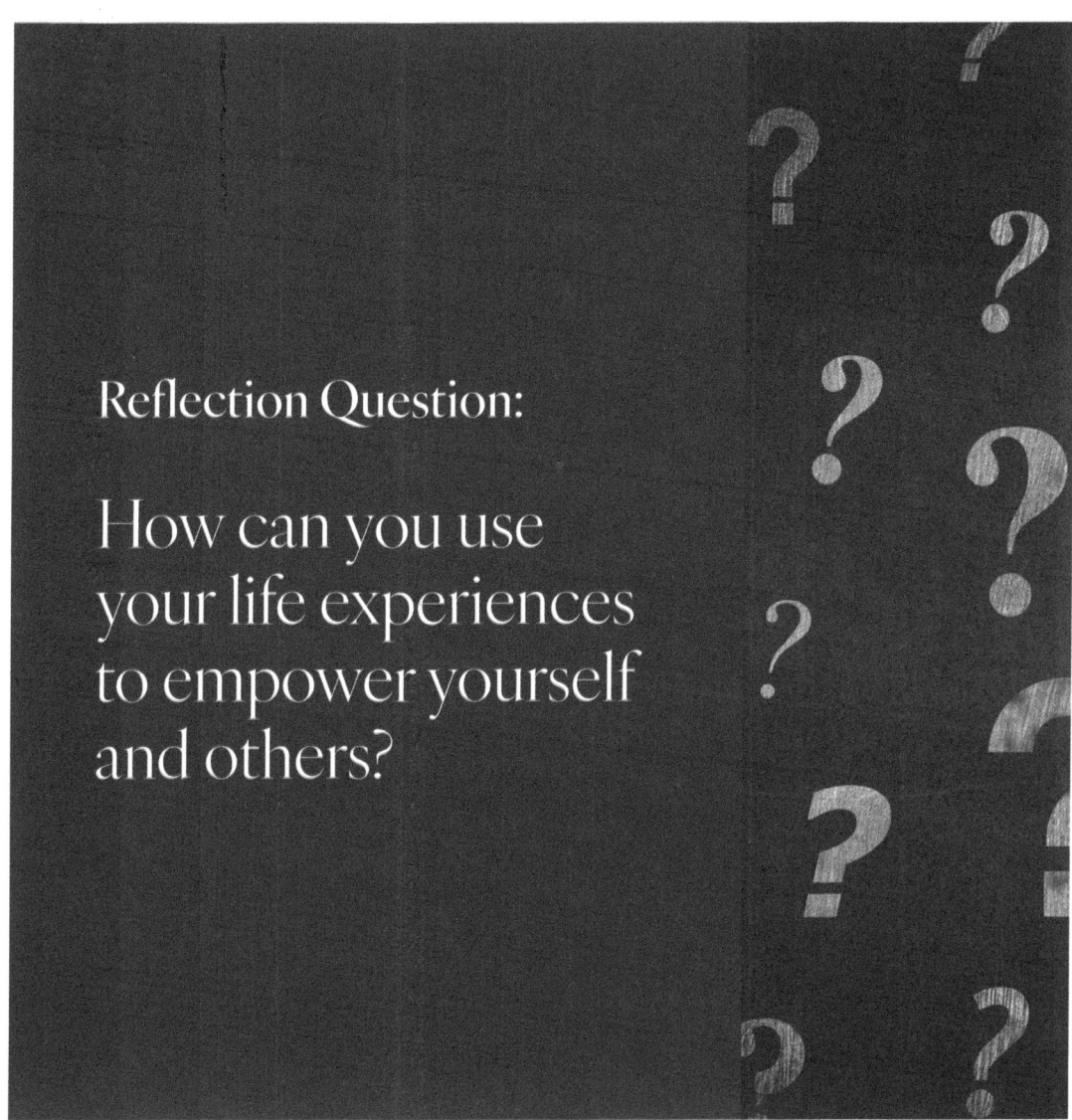

About the Author

Sheresse Winford is a determined woman who is living her newfound life helping and inspiring others in every way she can. She loves to travel, and she takes a solo trip every year to renew her spiritual strength.

Volunteering and being of service to the community is a very important part of Sheresse's life. She makes time for that when she isn't working at her full-time job in finance as a senior collection specialist and small business owner of Intouch Painting and Debris Removal.

Most importantly, Sheresse says, *"I love God with all my heart and soul."*

www.ingramcontent.com/pod-product-compliance
Lightning Source LLC
Chambersburg PA
CBHW061356010526
44107CB00012B/956